Mitzvah the Mutt

Also by Sylvia Rouss

CHILDREN'S PICTURE BOOKS

Sammy Spider Series
(Kar-Ben Publishing, a division of Lerner)

Sammy Spider's First Haggadah
Sammy Spider's First Hanukkah
Sammy Spider's First Tu B'Shevat
Sammy Spider's First Purim
Sammy Spider's First Passover
Sammy Spider's First Rosh Hashanah
Sammy Spider's First Shabbat
Sammy Spider's First Trip to Israel
Sammy Spider's First Sukkot
Sammy Spider's Hanukkah Fun Book
Sammy Spider's Passover Fun Book
Sammy Spider's Israel Fun Book
Sammy Spider's Shabbat Fun Book
Sammy Spider's First Shavuot
Sammy Spider's First Day of School

No Rules for Michael

Littlest Series
(Pitspopany, a division of Simcha Media)

The Littlest Maccabee
The Littlest Fish
The Littlest Frog
The Littlest Pair
The Littlest Candlesticks
The Littlest Tree

Tali's Jerusalem Scrapbook
God's World (Tikkun Olam)

Growing Up Jewish with Sarah Leah Jacobs Series
(Jonathan David Publishers)

My Baby Brother, What a Miracle!
Aaron's Bar Mitzvah

CHILDREN'S NON-FICTION

Reach for the Stars,
A Little Torah's Journey
(Pitspopany)

Fun with Jewish Holiday Rhymes
(URJ Books and Music)

Hanukkah Touch and Feel
(Kehot Publication Society)

Mitzvah the Mutt

by Sylvia Rouss

illustrations by Martha Rast

Yotzeret Publishing
St. Paul

PRINTING HISTORY
Yaldah Publishing paperback edition / June 2010
Yotzeret Publishing paperback edition / August 2011

Library of Congress Control Number: 2010928862

Publisher's Cataloging-in-Publication data
Rouss, Sylvia A.
    Mitzvah the Mutt / Sylvia Rouss , illustrated by Martha Rast.
    p. cm.
    ISBN 9781592871803 (pbk)
    ISBN 9781592873251 (ebook)
    SUMMARY : Mitzvah the Mutt is rescued by a Jewish family. His silly antics and humorous misinterpretations of the Jewish holidays charm his family.
    [1. Dogs-- Fiction. 2. Jews -- Fiction. 3. Family life -- Fiction. 4. Fasts and feasts --Judaism --Fiction. 5. Judaism --Customs and practices --Fiction. 6. Holidays --Fiction.] I. Rast, Martha. II. Title.

PZ7.R7622 Mit 2010
[E]—dc22   2010928862

                    9   8   7   6   5   4   3   2

For all my friends and family who love dogs, especially to my grandchildren, Hayden and Derek, who have four dogs, Cleo, Zoey, Emmy, and Ruby, and finally to Gretchen, the little rescue dog who inspired me to create the stories of Mitzvah the Mutt.
—S.R.

Contents

A Mitzvah for Shabbat

1

At the Pet Store

I was sitting in a cage outside Ruben's Pet Shop. The sign on the cage said, *Free to a good home*. I enjoyed watching all the activity on the noisy street: car horns honking, children laughing, people passing by on their way to work. Some stopped to look at me in the cage and chuckled. I've always been able to make people laugh or smile. I like to see them happy.

Last night Mr. Ruben told me, "Mutt," that's what he calls me, "the new apartment

Mitzvah the Mutt

I'm moving to doesn't allow animals so I have to find you a new home." I tried to assure him that I wasn't an animal. Animals are creatures in the zoo. I'm a dog. He didn't seem to understand me. That's the problem with people. They don't always understand us dogs because we communicate through our actions and an occasional bark. Dogs, on the other hand, understand most human words but there are a few I still can't figure out. Sometimes people look at me and say, "Woof-woof" or "Bow-wow" or "Ruf-ruf." I have no idea what they're talking about.

I like living with Mr. Ruben, who owns the pet shop. I spend most days at home while he goes to work. At night, he prepares my favorite food, hamburgers. He calls them burgers. He often talks to me about his day at the pet shop. He told me he sells "fancy-schmantsy" dogs. Those dogs have special papers that prove what kind of dog they are. Me, I don't need papers. Everyone seems to know I'm a mutt. That's because mutts are a special breed of dog. Each one of us is unique. There are no two mutts alike.

I'm a little dog with short brown hair. My ears are small and floppy. One hangs down a little while the other stands up. I have large brown eyes, a long nose, a crooked mouth and a tail that never stops wagging. I must have a good sense of humor because when Mr. Ruben takes me for a walk I always hear people say, "Look at that dog! He's so funny!" Then they roar with laughter.

This morning I went to work with Mr. Ruben. He scratched me behind my ears, then gently picked me up and put me inside the cage. He carefully wrote the sign and hung it

At the Pet Store

on the door of the cage. I guess he didn't want to sell me because, unlike the fancy-schmantsy dogs, I must be priceless. As some people passed by, they looked at me. A few said that silly word, "Woof-woof." I twisted my mouth into a lopsided grin. That made some of them smile and remark, "What a goofy dog!" I was actually enjoying myself, even though no one offered to take me home. I guess there are many people who feel they cannot provide the good home a dog like me deserves.

2

Finding Rachel

Later that day, I noticed a mother with two children, a boy and a girl, walking down the street. I watched as they entered Cohen's Bakery. When they came out, I saw that the mother had two twisted loaves of bread in the bag she was carrying. Each of the children was holding a cookie. "Yum! Those cookies look delicious," I said to myself.

Mr. Ruben only put water in my cage and I was feeling a little hungry. I hoped he would bring a burger to feed me for my dinner. The mother and both children stopped in front of a bookstore where the boy pointed at a book about dinosaurs. The mother wasn't listening when the girl said, "Mommy, I'm going into Schwartz's Toyland."

As the boy took a bite from his cookie, a shower of crumbs fell onto the sidewalk. I edged toward the front of the cage for a better look. My long nose accidentally bumped the door of the cage, which flew open. Without thinking, I jumped out and dashed over to the crumbs. I was busy licking up the last little bit, when I heard the mother shriek, "Where's Rachel? We have to find her!" I guess the mother wanted to let me know that if I found her daughter, she might also have crumbs for me.

"Maybe she went to the toy store?" the boy suggested. I trotted into Schwartz's Toyland with the mother, the boy following close behind. Immediately, I smelled the cookie, which led me to Rachel and her crumbs.

"See, Mommy, this is the board game I've been telling you about," she said, pointing to a large colorful box.

Mommy looked at Rachel and said, "Honey, I didn't know where you were. You frightened me! Please don't ever go off by yourself again."

"Sorry, Mommy, I thought you heard me say I was coming here," Rachel explained as I lapped up her cookie crumbs.

Mommy put down the bag she was carrying and scooped me up in her arms. "Thank you for helping me find Rachel," she said. I licked Mommy's face to thank her for helping me find

the crumbs and she began to laugh. "Where did you come from, little dog?"

I jumped out of her arms and she and the children followed me back to Ruben's Pet Shop. Mr. Ruben was in front of the shop looking for me. "There you are, Mutt," he shouted happily as we approached. Mommy told Mr. Ruben how I helped find Rachel. Suddenly, I was a hero! Mr. Ruben picked me up and placed me back in the cage. "I have a special treat for you," he said. Inside the cage, a big burger was waiting for me. As I ate the burger, the children watched and giggled with joy. I probably should have offered to share it with them but they had just finished their cookies and didn't look too hungry.

I heard their mother ask Mr. Ruben about me. "He's adorable," she said, "and I think he would be a perfect pet for Rachel and David. Would you let us take him home?"

Mr. Ruben smiled at the two children who were watching me swallow the last bite of my burger. "Yes, I think Mutt would be happy living with you." He helped Rachel and David select a red leash for me while Mommy purchased a bag of dog food. I'll have to let her know that I prefer burgers.

3

A New Name and a New Home

"Would you mind if we gave him a different name?" Mommy asked.

Mr. Ruben shook his head, "What name did you have in mind?" he inquired.

"I'd like to call him Mitzvah," she replied. "He looks like the kind of dog who wants to help people the way he helped me find Rachel."

Mr. Ruben nodded. "Yes, that's a good name for him." I guess he was remembering how I often helped him by eating the food that dropped onto his floor. I also helped him find his slippers because I never forgot where I left them after I finished chewing on them. I always barked to alert Mr. Ruben when someone came to his door, especially when it was someone who came to complain about the noise I made.

I also taught Mr. Ruben not to waste food. Once he left a plate of cheese and crackers on a table. I ate them up, of course. Now he's more careful about leaving food out.

I was surprised that no one bothered to ask me how I felt about the new name but I suppose Mitzvah is better than an ordinary name like Fido, Skipper or Spot.

Rachel and David promised to bring me back for visits as Mr. Ruben hugged me good-bye. Then I left with my new family. The children took turns holding my leash on the short walk to their house. Unlike Mr. Ruben's apartment, their house had a big yard with lots of trees. A small white picket fence surrounded the home. We entered the yard and, while David closed the gate, Rachel unfastened my leash. I ran towards a tree and found a tennis ball. I snapped it up and ran back to David, dropping it at his feet. He tossed the ball and I brought it back. "I want a turn!" said Rachel, picking up the ball and throwing it. They seemed to enjoy standing in one place, throwing a ball for me to retrieve.

4

Getting Ready for Shabbat

"It's time to prepare for Shabbat," Mommy announced. Mr. Ruben always spent Shabbat with friends so I was curious about this celebration. I followed my new family up the steps and inside the front door.

The house was huge! Mr. Ruben's place had been so small. I ran from room to room, wondering which one was going to be mine. When I entered the den, the children and their mother had placed a small rug near the fireplace.

"Here's where you can sleep, Mitzvah," Rachel proudly stated. I gulped. It was obvious this family never had a dog before. I would have to train them properly. Soon, they would realize that I liked to sleep on the couch or at the foot of a bed. I decided to be patient with them.

"Would you like some water, Mitzvah?" David asked.

I followed him into the kitchen. He set out a bowl of water while Rachel filled another dish with dog food. I drank the water but I wasn't interested in the dog food. Mommy began to prepare dinner. She put a chicken in the oven with potatoes and vegetables. She also began cooking a big pot of soup filled with tennis balls! I decided my new family was a little unusual.

Suddenly a stranger came walking up toward the house. I barked to alert the children and their mother. The stranger climbed the steps to the house and opened the door as if he owned the place. I ran up to him barking as fiercely as I could.

"Hi, Daddy," yelled David.

Oops! I realized this stranger *did* own the house. I stopped barking and rolled over on my back instead.

Rachel ran up and gave him a hug. "See our new dog!" she cried.

Daddy rubbed my stomach. "Where'd you find this mutt?" he asked. This man certainly knew about dogs. He recognized my breed immediately.

Mommy and the children told him the story about how we met. "Does he have all his shots?" Daddy asked.

That seemed like a strange question to me. I certainly didn't care if Daddy had all his shots.

Mommy nodded. "He was Mr. Ruben's dog and he took good care of him."

Yes, she was right. I had taken good care of Mr. Ruben.

Daddy seemed satisfied. I stood up on my hind legs and placed my front paws on Daddy's legs. I gave him my silly grin.

Daddy laughed, "This is a very funny dog! What's his name?"

"Mitzvah!" shouted David and Rachel.

"Great name! Not only did this dog perform a mitzvah today, but so have you, by providing him with a home!" Daddy responded approvingly. "Okay kids, let's help your mother set the table for Shabbat."

Rachel placed a pair of candlesticks on the table while David and Daddy set out the plates. "This challah smells delicious!" said

Mommy as she placed the two twisted loaves she bought earlier on the table.

Daddy placed a fancy cup next to the candlesticks and took a deep whiff. "Yes, it smells delicious," he agreed.

Mommy told Rachel and David, "Time to get dressed for Shabbat." I stayed and kept an eye on Daddy to make sure he didn't take a bite out of the challah.

5

Bubbie and Zaydie

I was startled by the ringing of the doorbell. Rachel and David, who were all dressed up, ran to answer the door. "Hi Bubbie, hi Zaydie," they greeted the two older people who entered the house. I guessed that they were the children's grandparents.

Bubbie and Zaydie hugged and kissed the children. Then Bubbie took her finger and wiped a smudge from David's nose. "You had a little *schmutz* on your nose," Bubbie told him.

I ran over to greet Bubbie and Zaydie too. As I placed my front paws on Bubbie's dress she started to push me away saying, "No, I don't want any schmutz on me!" I tried to let her know that my paws were clean. I had just wiped them on her dress. She didn't seem to understand as she continued to brush me away so I decided to greet Zaydie instead.

Zaydie held out his hand and let me lick it. Then I heard Bubbie say to him, "Go wash your hands." I guess she wanted to make sure Zaydie's hands were clean before I licked them.

Rachel and David told their grandparents how they found me. Zaydie scratched me behind the ears and Bubbie told him to wash his hands again. I wanted to let her know that his hands were probably still clean from the last time he washed them but she wouldn't let me come close to her.

6

Shabbat Shalom

As the family gathered around the table in the dining room, Rachel helped Mommy light the candles and sing a blessing. Next Daddy raised the fancy cup and handed it to David. "Would you like to sing the blessing over the Kiddush cup?" He asked. David nodded. Everyone sang a blessing over the challah. Mr. Ruben sometimes sang blessings too. I liked the sound but I didn't understand the words.

Mitzvah the Mutt

I followed Bubbie into the kitchen and watched Mommy ladle the soup with the tennis balls into bowls. As Bubbie carried the bowls to the dining table, one of the tennis balls fell to the floor. I wondered if she wanted to play with me. I snatched up the ball and placed it at her feet. I must have gripped it too tightly with my teeth because it didn't look like a tennis ball anymore. It looked like a shapeless blob. I hung my head since I knew Bubbie would probably be very angry with me.

Instead, she looked at me and chuckled. "What a good dog you are! You could have eaten that matzah ball, but you wanted to help me by bringing it back to me. Thank you, Mitzvah." Then she reached down and patted my head. "Go ahead, Mitzvah. You may eat the matzah ball."

Mitzvah the Mutt

While Bubbie went to wash her hands, I licked the tennis ball or matzah ball as she called it. It tasted good. I carefully took a bite. Soon I ate up the whole thing. I never knew there were edible tennis balls! During the rest of the meal, Bubbie made sure I had a taste of everything. The food tasted almost as good as Mr. Ruben's burgers.

That night when Bubbie and Zaydie were getting ready to leave, I followed the family to the door to say good night.

Everyone hugged and wished each other Shabbat Shalom. Zaydie scratched me behind the ears and said, "Shabbat Shalom, Mitzvah."

Bubbie looked at me and said, "Woof-woof." I gave her a crooked smile. I would miss Mr. Ruben but I had found a wonderful new family and I had enjoyed spending Shabbat with them.

Shabbat Shalom

As we stood on the front porch, I saw a sign on the door that I hadn't noticed before. Suddenly, I knew this was the perfect home for me. It had the last name of my new family: *The Bergers!*

A Miracle for Mitzvah

7

Fancy-Schmantsy Dogs

I've been living with the Berger family—
Mommy, Daddy, David and Rachel—for a while
now. I've become part of the family and I am
a very helpful dog. I lick up spills, I announce
the arrival of guests by barking loudly, and I
help with the gardening by digging holes in the
flowerbed. I only track dirt into the entryway.
By the time I reach the rest of the house, my
paws are nice and clean.

Mitzvah the Mutt

Although I miss Mr. Ruben, I like my new family. Sometimes I take Mommy and the children for a walk to visit Mr. Ruben at his pet shop. Rachel and David enjoy looking at all the fancy-schmantsy dogs. It helps them appreciate what a special dog I am.

"Look at the poodles!" I've heard Rachel say.

David will point at other dogs and remark, "Those are Cocker Spaniels."

That's the problem with fancy-schmantsy dogs. Each breed has dogs that look alike. There is no other dog at the pet shop that looks like me with my brown hair, large dark eyes, long nose, lopsided mouth and short floppy ears—one stands up while the other hangs down.

Each time before we leave, Mr. Ruben gives me my favorite treat—burgers—just like the name of my new family. When I came to live with the Bergers, I had to train them because they had never lived with a dog before. At first, they wanted me to sleep on a rug near the fireplace but they soon learned that during the day, I prefer to sleep on the couch and at night, I like to sleep at the foot of David's or Rachel's bed.

8

Can't Teach an Old Dog New Tricks

Tonight, Bubbie and Zaydie, the children's grandparents, are coming over to visit while Mommy and Daddy go out for dinner. I wonder if they are going to Mr. Ruben's pet shop for burgers. I hope they bring home a doggy bag for me.

David, Rachel and I ran to the door when Bubbie and Zaydie arrived. Bubbie hugged and kissed her grandchildren. I barked and waited for my hug and kiss but Bubbie gave me her usual greeting, "Woof, woof, Mitzvah." Although I understand most human words, I still have no idea what that means. Zaydie gave the children a bear hug and then reached down to pet me. I heard Bubbie say to him, "Go wash your hands!" She is very thoughtful and always reminds Zaydie and the children to wash their hands when they touch me. I think she wants to make sure I don't get any germs.

Everyone waved good-bye as Mommy and Daddy left, and then we headed for the family room. Bubbie brushed the couch with her hand and said, "Mitzvah, your hair is all over the place." I tried to assure her that, even though I shed, my hair grows back. I think she is concerned because Zaydie shed the hair on his head and it has never grown back. As she settled onto the couch cushion, I jumped up to sit next to her. "Dogs don't belong on the furniture!" she announced.

As hard as I have tried, I have not been able to train Bubbie. There is a saying, "You can't teach an old dog new tricks." Maybe that also applies to Bubbie.

9

Dreidels

I hopped onto Zaydie's lap. Bubbie looked at him and said, "You're going to have dog hair all over you." I was puzzled. Did she really think Zaydie would start growing dog hair on his body?

Zaydie didn't seem to care. He asked Rachel and David, "Do you know what holiday we will begin celebrating tomorrow night?"

"Hanukkah!" they both cried.

"Yes." Zaydie nodded, reaching into his pocket and pulling out two small tops. He gave the blue one to Rachel and the yellow one to David. "Time to start practicing," he said with a grin.

"Thanks for the dreidel, Zaydie!" David exclaimed

"Let's play," said Rachel. The children sat on the floor and began spinning the driedels. I ran over to join them. First, I pounced on David's dreidel and then on Rachel's.

"Mitzvah! That's not how you play the game!" Rachel laughed.

"You have to wait until they stop spinning!" David added.

I was confused. That's like throwing a ball and not wanting me to fetch it. What a ridiculous game. I watched as the children continued playing.

10

A New Game

My ears perked up to a *click-click* sound coming from the couch. Bubbie was playing a game I'd never seen before. She held two long needles in her hands. Attached to the needles was a string of yarn. At the end of the string was a ball made entirely of yarn!

I watched her continue to click the needles together. Zaydie was reading a book and so I decided to play with Bubbie instead. I grabbed the ball of yarn and ran out of the family room. Bubbie chased after me yelling, "Stop, Mitzvah, stop!"

This game was fun! David and Rachel joined in the chase as Zaydie began laughing. Everyone was having such a good time. I love making my family happy. I stopped when David grabbed my collar and Rachel snatched the ball of yarn from my mouth and handed it to Bubbie. It must be Bubbie's turn, I thought. I waited for her to put the ball of yarn in her mouth and begin running.

She looked at me and shook her finger. "That's my knitting, Mitzvah!" she scolded. "I'm making Hanukkah gifts for the family!" I decided that Bubbie wanted to play alone, just like David and Rachel, so I spent the rest of the evening on Zaydie's lap.

11

Latkes

The next afternoon I watched Rachel help Mommy polish a silver menorah. I remember Mr. Ruben's was made out of clay and he never had to polish it. "This menorah has been in my family for years," Mommy told Rachel. I felt sad for Mommy. The menorah looked old and used. Maybe Daddy will buy her a new one made out of clay.

Latkes

Later when Daddy came home, he did not have a new menorah for Mommy. Instead, he brought home a box of money.

I heard David exclaim, "Thanks! I love to eat Hanukkah gelt!" This does not surprise me. My new family is a bit unusual. I've seen them cook tennis balls in water, which they call matzah ball soup. I actually ate the edible tennis balls and, I must admit, they were delicious. I'm not so sure about eating gold coins, though.

"When is Bubbie coming over to make her famous latkes?" asked Daddy.

"She and Zaydie should be here at any moment," answered Mommy.

I heard the familiar footsteps approaching the front door and began barking. Mommy and Daddy opened the door for Bubbie and Zaydie. When Bubbie handed Mommy an armful of packages, I was shocked to see that Bubbie had grown dog hair overnight!

I was relieved when Daddy said, "Let me take your coat," and Bubbie unbuttoned her furry jacket. Whew! It was just clothing. I quickly moved as Daddy brushed by me. I didn't want to get any of that hair on me!

David and Rachel came running. "Can we help make latkes?" they both cried.

"Of course you can, but first you have to wash your hands," replied Bubbie.

I wanted to make latkes too so I wiped my paws on the rug to make sure they were clean and then I followed Bubbie into the kitchen. "First, we need to grate the potatoes," Bubbie explained while Rachel and David dried their hands.

I watched Bubbie peel the potatoes. Then, Rachel and David took turns grating them.

When a piece of potato dropped on the floor, I snapped it up. Yuck! It tasted worse than dog food. I drank some water from my bowl to get rid of the taste.

Bubbie added eggs, flour and salt to the potato mixture. Then she put some oil in a frying pan and placed it on the stove. She let Rachel and David drop spoonfuls of the mixture into the sizzling oil. After they were finished cooking, Bubbie let each of the children sample the latkes before she carried a plateful into the dining room. I was glad Bubbie didn't offer me a taste. Usually, I like eating table scraps. Tonight, I would settle for dog food. I knew anything would be better than latkes.

"Zaydie likes sour cream on his latkes," Rachel said taking a carton of sour cream from the refrigerator.

Latkes

"Yes." David nodded. "And I'll bring the applesauce for Mommy." I wasn't surprised. Mommy and Zaydie probably wanted to cover up the bad taste of the latkes.

12

Hanukkah Gifts

I followed the children into the dining room. Mommy and Daddy had already set the table. I noticed that the menorah in the center of the table only had two candles in it, one tall one in the middle and one on the end. I also saw the box filled with gold coins.

Everyone sat around the table. I curled up on the floor near Zaydie's chair as he told the story of Hanukkah. "Judah Maccabee led the Jewish people in a revolt against King

Hanukkah Gifts

Antiochus, who wouldn't let them pray in the Holy Temple. After they won the war, they searched for oil to relight the Temple menorah."

I wished I'd been there, I thought. I could have sniffed out the oil immediately.

Zaydie continued, "They found a tiny bit of oil that they thought would last for only one day but it lasted for eight. It was a wonderful miracle! That's why we celebrate Hanukkah for eight nights. Each night, we use the Shamash, the tall candle in the menorah, to light one more candle. On the last night, we light all eight."

I watched Mommy light the first candle while everyone sang the blessings for Hanukkah.

I yelped along with Rachel and David when they sang a song about dreidels. Bubbie covered her ears. I think she enjoyed our singing so much, she wanted to capture the sound.

After we finished, Rachel asked, "Bubbie, can we open our gifts before dinner?"

"Of course you can." Bubbie beamed as she reached for the gifts that had been placed on a nearby table.

I watched Mommy unwrap a pair of slippers that Bubbie had knitted. I recognized the yarn. Daddy got a scarf and Rachel got mittens.

Then David opened his present. Inside was a cone-shaped hat with a big pom-pom on top. I rolled onto my back and chuckled to myself. It looked so silly. David politely tried it on but it was too small.

Suddenly, Bubbie laughed. "Oh David, that isn't for you." She handed him another package. "I made you mittens like Rachel's. That adorable hat is for Mitzvah."

I gulped! Bubbie took the hat and before I could get away she tied it under my chin. "Happy Hanukkah, Mitzvah!" she said. "When you ran off with my ball of yarn yesterday, I knew it was your way of telling me you wanted me to knit something for you. Woof-woof."

Everyone thanked Bubbie for the gifts. I tried to remove my hat but Bubbie had tied it firmly in place. David took a gold coin and peeled away the foil. Inside was chocolate. He popped the entire piece of edible money into his mouth. "Yum!" he exclaimed.

"David, make sure Mitzvah doesn't eat gelt. It might make him sick," Daddy cautioned as David unwrapped another piece and ate it. He seemed to enjoy eating food that made me sick.

13

The Miracle

"I've got something for you, Mitzvah," Bubbie suddenly announced. She took a latke and put it on the floor near my feet. I leaned forward and sniffed it, as the pom-pom on my hat dangled between my eyes.

I heard Daddy say, "Go ahead, Mitzvah, you'll like it."

"It's better than burgers," added David.

"Maybe Mitzvah would like applesauce or sour cream on his latke," suggested Zaydie.

Mitzvah the Mutt

"Plain is best," insisted Rachel.

I looked up at Mommy who smiled back at me and said, "Try it, Mitzvah."

What could I do? Everyone was watching me. I gave them a crooked grin. Then, I closed my eyes and took a small bite. I chewed slowly. "Not bad," I said to myself. I took another bite. Bubbie's latkes were delicious! I swallowed the last little bit.

Bubbie looked pleased. "I see you like my latkes," she said, giving me another one.

I was amazed! How did those disgusting potatoes turn into tasty treats when Bubbie fried them in oil? Suddenly, I understood: Hanukkah is the holiday that celebrates the *miracle of the oil!*

Dayenu, Mitzvah, Dayenu

14

A Walk on a Spring Day

All this past week, my new family, the Berger's, have been preparing for Passover. They've been cleaning and scrubbing the house. They've removed the bagels and bread, the cereals and pastas, and the cookies and cakes. And last night they changed their dishes. I even got a new dog dish.

My previous owner, Mr. Ruben, always had me assist him. He would remove a few items from his cupboards while I patiently waited.

Mitzvah the Mutt

There usually wasn't that much but whatever Mr. Ruben couldn't keep for the holiday he would pass over to me and I would eat it up. I figured that's why he called it Passover.

This morning Rachel announced, "Tonight is the Seder, Mitzvah. You will really enjoy it." I'd never been to a Seder because Mr. Ruben always went to a friend's home. I stood up on my hind legs to show Rachel how excited I was. Just then, David entered the room with my leash in his hand.

"It's a beautiful spring day, Rachel. Let's take Mitzvah for a walk." As we stepped out the door we saw our new neighbor, Mrs. Friedman, taking a walk with her French poodle, Fifi. Mrs. Friedman's dog is a fancy-schmantsy dog, similar to those at Ruben's Pet Shop. She looks the same as every other poodle I've seen. I am glad that there is no other dog that looks exactly like me, with my long nose, big brown eyes, a crooked mouth and small floppy ears. That's what makes me special!

I wagged my tail at Mrs. Friedman and Fifi in a friendly greeting as we approached.

"Good morning," said Rachel and David.

"Hello," answered Mrs. Friedman, pulling Fifi's leash closer to her. Fifi looked as if she had just been to the dog groomer. Her hair was clipped and brushed. She wore a bright pink ribbon on her head. Many fancy-schmantsy dogs wear bows or ribbons. It helps their owners tell them apart. "What kind of dog is that?" asked Mrs. Friedman, looking at me and scratching her head.

"He's a mutt!" Rachel proudly replied.

"We call him Mitzvah," David added.

"Does he have fleas?" Mrs. Friedman inquired.

A Walk on a Spring Day

Hey, I'm not the one scratching my head, I thought as I watched Mrs. Friedman. Abruptly, she stopped scratching and picked up Fifi.

"She gets nervous around other dogs," she explained.

I get nervous around people who might have fleas, I thought, keeping my distance from Mrs. Friedman.

"I'm sure Mitzvah doesn't have any fleas," David stated, but Mrs. Friedman seemed unconvinced.

15

Crossing the Red Sea

We continued on our walk and I noticed several puddles on the sidewalk from the last spring storm. Occasionally a fallen tree branch blocked our way. I picked up a small broken twig with my mouth and led the children around the branches and through the puddles.

"I wonder if Mitzvah is pretending to be Moses leading us through the Red Sea," Rachel laughed.

Crossing the Red Sea

I'd never met Moses. He must be someone else's dog. I splashed through another deep dirty puddle. It wasn't red but it was a beautiful shade of brown. Mud and water clung to my fur. I was having a great time! If puddles are this much fun, I can only imagine what fun an entire sea would be. I hoped some day I'd get to meet Moses and we could run through puddles together.

Rachel and David stopped in front of Mr. and Mrs. Bloom's house. Mrs. Bloom was busy planting flower seeds, while Mr. Bloom was hanging a wooden box on a tree branch. I noticed their baby boy, Josh, sitting in a stroller, eating a banana.

"Hi Rachel and David," said Mr. Bloom. "Would you children like to put some bird seed in the birdhouse?"

Rachel and David nodded and took a handful of seeds. I stared at the tiny kernels and shook my head with wonder. I had always thought that birds hatch from eggs. I never knew they grew from seeds the way flowers do!

Suddenly, I heard baby Josh shouting, "Doggie!" Then he began to giggle. David and Rachel walked me over to the baby so he could pet me. Josh reached out and pulled one of my ears. I tried to get away but then he grabbed my tail.

Mrs. Bloom looked alarmed and said, "Josh, you need to be gentle. That hurts the doggie." Then she said to David and Rachel, "Sorry, Josh isn't used to dogs. I hope he doesn't bite."

Uh-oh, I thought. Why didn't Mrs. Bloom warn us earlier? I noticed that Josh had finished eating the banana. I didn't want him to start chomping on me! When I felt Josh loosen his grip, I dashed away as far as my leash allowed.

Josh laughed and yelled, "Doggie run!"

Rachel and David waved goodbye to the Blooms as I dragged them down the street back to our house.

16

A Bath Before Seder

Bubbie and Zaydie were just pulling into the driveway. I ran with David and Rachel to greet them. Bubbie and Zaydie hugged and kissed the children. I held out my paw and Zaydie shook it.

"Wash your hands," Bubbie reminded him as she always does. She doesn't want people to touch me unless their hands are clean. I lifted my paw for her to shake but she ignored it. Maybe she wanted to wash her hands first, too. I noticed Bubbie's freshly styled hair and guessed that she had recently been clipped and groomed like Fifi.

As Zaydie walked up the steps and into the house, Bubbie frowned at my still-wet fur and exclaimed, "Mitzvah, you look as if you could use a bath before tonight's Seder. And it will make you smell better too," she added.

I was shocked! I thought that my long nose had always been able to smell perfectly well. I never knew that taking a bath would improve my sniffing ability.

I waited with Bubbie while Rachel and David ran to get my tub and shampoo. After David filled the tub with water from the garden hose, he lifted me in and shampooed my fur. Bubbie watched to make sure David didn't miss a spot. Rachel used the garden hose to rinse off the suds. Bubbie smiled at me approvingly. "You look and smell so much better, Mitzvah."

David and Rachel nodded in agreement.

I gazed up at Bubbie's cheerful face and wanted to do something nice for her. Perhaps she would enjoy a bath. I shook my head and body as hard as I could. Water sprayed everywhere. Bubbie was soaked. She no longer seemed happy. Her freshly groomed hair hung down into her eyes. She brushed it away and said, "Mitzvah, you've ruined my hairdo!"

I tried to let Bubbie know that all she needed to do was shake her head the way I did and she would be dry. I gave her another demonstration.

Bubbie didn't seem to understand. "No, Mitzvah!" she yelled and then she rushed into the house. I wanted to tell Bubbie not to be upset because now she would smell better too.

Mitzvah the Mutt

I waited to enter the house with David and Rachel. I took a deep whiff. My nose inhaled the wonderful cooking aromas. Bubbie was right! I *was* able to smell better!

I found Bubbie helping Mommy in the kitchen. Bubbie was stirring the soup with the edible tennis balls that the family calls matzah balls. Her hair had dried and it still looked nice. She smiled at Mommy and said, "This smells delicious!"

I guess the bath I'd given Bubbie had worked for her sniffing ability as well.

17

The Seder Plate

I watched Daddy carry a stack of plates into the dining room. "I'll set the table for the Seder," he told Mommy.

Bubbie came in with an armful of books. "I'll place a haggadah next to each plate," she said.

"Can we help too?" asked David and Rachel as they entered the room.

Rachel was holding a large plate. "Here's the Seder plate I made at school!" she proudly announced. Zaydie helped the children fill the large plate with a variety of unusual foods. Rachel let me taste the haroset.

"You'll like this, Mitzvah," she said. She was right. The haroset tasted almost as good as the burgers I ate when I lived with Mr. Ruben. Burgers are still my favorite food.

Next, Zaydie added some green weeds and a burnt egg to the plate, while David added a bone. He called it the shank bone. I hoped it was for me.

Finally, Rachel placed something on the plate that had a strong smell and looked very interesting. When a small piece fell to the ground, I eagerly snapped it up.

"No, Mitzvah!" Rachel shouted. "That's maror! You won't like it!"

Her warning was too late. My mouth was on fire. I ran to drink water from my bowl. It

didn't help. My tongue was still burning. I ran around in circles, and then took another drink of water. My eyes were watering and my nose was twitching.

"Tsk, tsk, tsk," Bubbie clicked her tongue. She placed a matzah ball near my feet. "Here, Mitzvah, eat this. It might help you get rid of the taste."

I swallowed the matzah ball and felt much better. I thanked Bubbie with a lopsided grin.

"Woof-woof," she said. I can understand most things Bubbie says but that is one word that still puzzles me.

18

Something Special

"Time to get dressed for the Seder," Mommy announced as David and Rachel ran off to put on their holiday clothes.

"I have something special for you to wear, Mitzvah," cooed Bubbie.

Oh no, I thought. I didn't want another hat like the one she made me for Hanukkah.

She reached into her pocket, pulled out a bright blue bow tie and clipped it around my neck. "You look very handsome now," she noted. I wanted to tell Bubbie that I didn't want to look like a fancy-schmantsy dog when the doorbell rang.

Bubbie answered the door. Mr. and Mrs. Bloom had come with baby Josh. Mrs. Bloom smiled at Bubbie and handed her a large bouquet of flowers. "These are for the Seder table."

Mr. Bloom held out a large rubber bone. "We brought a gift for you, Mitzvah."

I wasn't sure what to do. Did he expect me to eat it? As I politely grasped the bone in my jaws, it made a loud squeaking noise. Josh squealed with delight. I thought about offering it to him. Maybe he would enjoy chewing on it for a while.

Suddenly, the doorbell rang again. Zaydie opened the door and there stood Mr. Ruben, my previous owner, holding a bottle of wine and a small paper bag. "Hello, Mitzvah," he said. "The Bergers invited me to the Seder. I have a little something for you," he continued, reaching into the bag and pulling out a burger. "It's made with matzah meal," Mr. Ruben told Bubbie. I dropped the rubber bone and gulped down the entire burger. I thanked Mr. Rubin with a crooked smile.

Once more, I heard the doorbell. This time Mommy and Daddy answered it. Mrs. Friedman entered the house with a box of candy and a small package. I did not see Fifi. "Thank you for the invitation to the Seder," she exclaimed. "Oh, Mitzvah, here's a present for you," she said opening the package. "It's a flea collar. Let me put it around your neck." She reached down and placed the flea collar underneath my bow tie. How thoughtful of her! I guess she didn't want me to get her fleas.

Mitzvah the Mutt

Just then, Rachel and David came to greet the guests. Rachel wore a pretty pale blue dress and David had on a bright blue bow tie that matched mine. Mommy and Daddy invited everyone into the dining room.

19

Dayenu

I listened as Zaydie began reading from one of the books Bubbie had called a Haggadah. He held up the flat cracker that Mr. Ruben had once told me was matzah. Zaydie broke it in half. He wrapped one of the broken halves in a napkin and Bubbie hid it. She told Rachel and David, "After the meal you may hunt for the afikoman. I think Bubbie likes to confuse me. She just called the matzah the afikoman. But then she also says, "Woof, woof." I guess I'll never understand her.

Zaydie asked David and Rachel to sing the four questions. They started singing in words I couldn't understand. Were they trying to confuse me like Bubbie? I hoped one of the questions was, "When is dinner?" My stomach growled and I thought about hunting for the afikommen, but when I saw Bubbie watching me, I changed my mind.

The Berger family and their guests took turns reading from the Haggadah. I heard that the Jewish people were slaves for Pharaoh in a place called Egypt. Pharaoh made them work very hard. One day, Moses, their leader, demanded that Pharaoh let the Jewish people go, but Pharaoh refused. Then bad things called plagues happened. I glanced at Mrs.

Friedman and wondered if there had been a
plague of fleas.

Finally, Pharaoh agreed to let them leave.
Moses took the Jewish people out of Egypt.
When they got to the Red Sea, he parted the
waters so everyone could cross. I glimpsed at
David's Haggadah and saw a picture of Moses.
He was a man, not a dog as I had previously
thought. Somehow, I couldn't imagine him
splashing through puddles with me. During
the reading of the Haggadah, everyone ate
some of the foods on the Seder plate. I made
sure to stay away from the maror.

Just before the meal, David and Rachel
led the others in a song. They kept singing
"Dayenu." I started howling and Bubbie looked
at me and said, "Dayenu, that's enough." I
guess Bubbie was ready to eat.

Mitzvah the Mutt

My mouth watered when Bubbie served the matzah ball soup. Next, Mommy offered everyone gefilte fish. It didn't look like any fish I'd ever seen. Daddy brought brisket to the table and Mommy brought a large platter of chicken. There was also matzah kugel, broccoli, and cooked carrots. I was allowed to sample everything. Then it was time to help Rachel and David find the afikommen. Now that I smelled better, I found it immediately. Zaydie gave each of the children a storybook as a prize. I got a pat on the head.

Soon it was time for dessert. Bubbie brought in a cake. "I made it from scratch with matzah meal." I figured itchy Mrs. Friedman would enjoy scratchy cake and I hoped there would be a piece left for me. David gave me a small slice. I ate it even though I felt stuffed! When I finished I could barely walk. I realized

if I'd only eaten the matzah ball and not the gefilte fish, it would have been enough. If I'd only eaten the brisket and not the chicken, it would have been enough. If I'd only eaten the carrots and not the kugel, it would have been enough. If I'd only eaten dinner and not dessert, it would have been enough.

Bubbie smiled at me, "Would you like anything else, Mitzvah?" she asked.

I looked at Bubbie and thought, Dayenu— *that's enough!*

About the Author

Sylvia Rouss is the award-winning author and early childhood educator who created the popular *Sammy Spider* and *The Littlest* books. Even with her success as an author, Sylvia has not given up what she loves most, teaching. She is currently a preschool teacher in Los Angeles, California, and says that she is "inspired by the children in my classroom." Sylvia also received awards as an educator and she conducts seminars for parents and teachers. She is a featured author and lecturer at book fairs throughout the United States and Israel. Visit her on the web at www.sylviarouss.com.

About the Illustrator

Martha Rast was born and raised in Minneapolis, Minnesota, in spite of her intolerance to cold weather. She attended both The School of the Art Institute of Chicago, and the Minneapolis College of Art and Design, where she studied for her BFA. in Painting and Drawing, and her professional certificate in Art Education. Martha has taught art in Chicago, Minneapolis, and St. Paul to all ages, and loves teaching workshops. She continues to work as a fine artist in oil paints, encaustic, and assemblage and shows her work in a variety of venues in both the Midwest and Southwest. She is inspired by her children and the wonder of nature around her.